Reading Essen...
in Science

AMAZING SPACE

Telescopes
Exploring the Beyond

ELLEN HOPKINS

PERFECTION LEARNING®

Editorial Director: Susan C. Thies
Editor: Judith A. Bates
Design Director: Randy Messer
Book Design: Tobi S. Cunningham, Jill Kline
Cover Design: Mike Aspengren

A special thanks to Kristin Mandsager, instructor of physics
and astronomy at North Iowa Area Community College, for
his scientific review of the book.

IMAGE CREDITS
COVER: photos.com, NASA, NOAO
©Roger Ressmeyer/CORBIS: pp. 4–5; ©Bettmann/CORBIS: pp. 8, 9; ©Bob
Rowan; Progressive Image/CORBIS: p. 22; Digital image ©1996 CORBIS;
Original image courtesy of NASA/CORBIS: p. 27; ©CORBIS SYGMA: p. 30

Comstock Images: pp. 2–3; NASA: pp. 1, 6, 17, 23, 24, 25 (bottom), 28–29, 31,
34, 36, 37, 38, 39, 40; NRAO/AUI/NSF: pp. 18, 19, 20; NOAO/AURA/NSF:
pp. 14, 16, 26, 46, 48; ArtToday (arttoday.com): p. 15; Corel: pp. 6–7
(background), 10–11 (background), 14–15 (background), 18–19 (background),
22–23 (background), 26–27 (background), 32–33 (background); Photos.com:
pp. 25 (top), 33, 41, 42–43, 44–46, 47; PLC images: pp. 7, 10–11, 12, 13, 21

Printed in the United States of America. For information, contact
Perfection Learning® Corporation,
1000 North Second Avenue, P.O. Box 500,
Logan, Iowa 51546-0500.
Tel: 1-800-831-4190 • Fax: 1-800-543-2745
perfectionlearning.com

2 3 4 5 6 7 BA 10 09 08 07 06 05

Paperback ISBN 0-7891-6078-1

Reinforced Library Binding ISBN 0-7569-4448-1

Table of Contents

The Very Large Array consists of 27 radio telescopes on the Plains of San Agustin, 50 miles west of Socorro, New Mexico. Each telescope's dish is 82 feet in diameter. The data from the telescopes is combined electronically to equal a telescope with a dish 422 feet in diameter. The telescopes are mounted on tracks so they can be placed in several formations.

Exploring the Beyond

Space is a big place. A very big place. Our own little neighborhood, the Milky Way Galaxy, is almost too vast to imagine. Stars bigger than our Sun appear as tiny points of light in the night sky. Planets in our own solar system look no bigger—nor smaller—no matter where we stand on Earth. Comets shoot across the sky, and asteroids sometimes fall through our atmosphere and crash-land to form craters.

Two or three thousand years ago, people didn't know that stars were giant balls of burning gas or that planets orbited the Sun. They had no clue that comets were made of ice or that asteroids were leftovers from the birth of the solar system. All they knew was what they could see with their eyes—or what they could imagine.

But they wanted to know more. With one very special invention, and a relatively simple one at that, people soon gained a universe of knowledge.

chapter 1

Glimpsing the Beyond

Light Energy and Telescopes

The invention that provided people an up close view of the heavens was the telescope. The word *telescope* comes from the Greek words *tele*, meaning "from afar" and *skopos*, meaning "viewer."

There are many types of telescopes. They all work by gathering light and other kinds of **electromagnetic radiation** from distant objects. Then the telescopes focus the energy and create images of distant objects that look larger than they do using only your eye. Does that sound complicated? It's really not.

Electromagnetic radiation is a form of energy. It comes to us as waves that move through space at the **speed of light**, spreading out as they go. There are many types of energy waves. Together, they make up the electromagnetic (EM) **spectrum**.

The Hubble Space Telescope captured this image of Mars on June 26, 2001. Mars was about 43 million miles from Earth, the closest it has ever been to Earth since 1988.

Electromagnetic Spectrum

Some EM waves have low energy, while others have high energy. Only very hot, very high-energy objects like stars can **emit** waves on the high-energy end of the EM spectrum. Here is how the spectrum looks—from low energy (long **wavelengths**) to high energy (short wavelengths).

- Radio waves are like those that travel from transmitters at radio or TV stations to receivers that re-create music or movies in homes.

- Microwaves are used to transmit information just like radio waves. They are also the waves that are emitted to bounce off airplanes in radar systems. Microwave ovens are so named because they use microwaves to heat food.

- Infrared waves have a little less energy than light and cannot be seen with your eyes. But you can feel them as warmth against your skin. Besides sending out light waves, the Sun emits infrared waves, which can burn the inside of your eyes. That's why you should never look directly at the Sun without something to remove the infrared waves.

- Light waves are the only ones visible to the human eye.

- Ultraviolet (UV) radiation is emitted from very hot objects. It is what the Sun (and other stars) emits that can give us a sunburn.

- X rays are what doctors use to look inside our bodies. Ultrahot gases in space also emit X rays.

- Gamma rays come from reactions within and between **nuclei**. Humans cause some of these reactions, such as in nuclear reactors. Others occur in nature without human help. Some elements that naturally emit gamma rays include radium, thorium, and uranium.

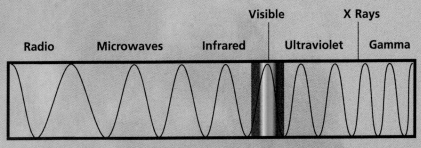

7

Many different kinds of telescopes have been created to view radiation from all parts of the EM spectrum. This radiation can be turned into images of the objects that emitted the waves. Radio, microwave, infrared, light, and UV waves can be focused by **reflecting** the waves off a curved surface. Infrared, light, and UV waves can be focused by **refracting**, or bending, them with glass lenses. Gamma and X rays take special instruments.

Different kinds of telescopes are used for viewing different types of radiation. The most common is the **optical** telescope. This was the first telescope to be developed. It used mirrors and/or lenses to gather visible light radiation.

> ### What Is a Lens?
>
> A lens is a clear, curved piece of material, usually glass, that bends rays of light to form an image. A **concave** lens is thicker in the middle and causes light to spread out. A **convex** lens is thinner in the middle and causes light to come together.

Two Men and Their Telescopes

So who was the first person to figure out that using lenses could magnify distant objects? Most people say Hans Lippershey. Others claim it was Galileo. We do know that lenses probably were used, in one form or another, long before the early 1600s when Galileo and Lippershey were busy inventing things.

The Egyptians made glass as early as 3500 B.C. In the 3rd century B.C., an Egyptian mathematician named Euclid wrote about the refraction and reflection of light. Archaeologists have dug up simple lenses in Egypt dating to 2000 B.C.

About 1000 A.D., an Arab physicist, Alhazen, was experimenting with lenses and reflection. Unlike other scientists of his time, Alhazen correctly believed that objects are seen by the light they reflect, not by light coming out of the eye.

Euclid

Hans Lippershey (1570–1619) is considered by most scholars to be the inventor of the telescope. He was a Dutch eyeglass maker.

Lippershey

According to an old tale, Lippershey saw his children playing in his workshop. When the children looked through two of Papa Lippershey's lenses, a weather vane on a nearby building looked larger and clearer.

Whether or not his children had anything to do with his invention, Lippershey did hold two lenses a certain distance apart and then sight through them. In fact, he built on the idea by putting a tube between the two lenses to create a telescope. Lippershey called his invention a *kijker*, which means "looker" in Dutch.

Galileo Galilei (1564–1642) taught mathematics and astronomy at the University of Pisa in Italy. In the summer of 1609, Galileo heard about a spyglass made in Holland. Using his own knowledge of light and lenses, Galileo built a series of telescopes with better optical performances than the Dutch model.

Galileo Galilei

Galileo's telescope significantly advanced scientific knowledge. It also sent the world reeling by proving the universe did not revolve around an unmoving Earth.

Galileo's *The Starry Messenger* was published in Venice in 1610. In it, Galileo outlined the incredible discoveries he had made with his telescopes.
- The Moon's surface was not smooth, but had mountains and craters.
- Jupiter had four major moons.
- The Milky Way was made up of numerous stars.
- Venus underwent a sequence of phases and changes in **apparent** size that were consistent with an orbit around the Sun and not consistent with an orbit around Earth, as had been assumed.

chapter 2

Lenses and Mirrors

Okay, to understand how a telescope works, you must first understand how a lens works.

Try This!

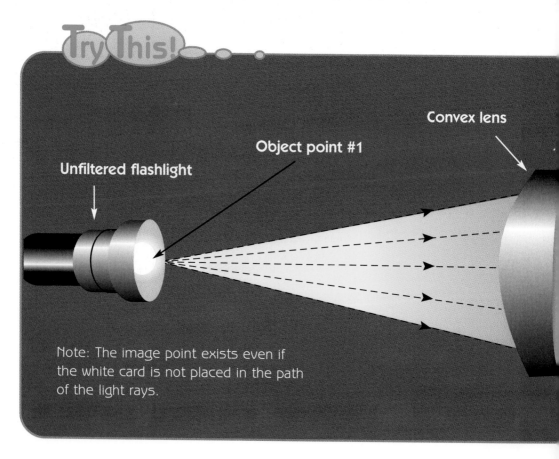

Convex lens

Object point #1

Unfiltered flashlight

Note: The image point exists even if the white card is not placed in the path of the light rays.

Place a flashlight on a distant table in a dark room. Hold a convex lens in one hand and a white index card in the other and line them up. Focus the light of the flashlight on the card. Do you see a small point of light on the card? Every ray coming from a point of light, the object point, that strikes the face of the lens is bent so that all such rays cross at a single point on the other side of the lens. This is the image point.

Next, move the card slightly closer to the lens. Do you see a fuzzy circle of light instead of a tiny point? The same thing should occur when you move the card slightly farther from the lens. These could be called *circles of confusion*. Putting the index card too close results in the rays hitting the card before they have a chance to come together. Putting the card too far from the lens results in the rays hitting the card after they have come together and have begun to spread apart from one another. This is called *blurring*.

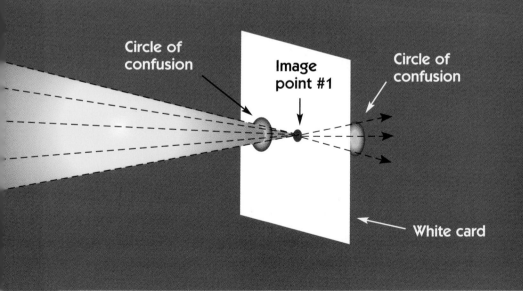

Circle of confusion

Image point #1

Circle of confusion

White card

Refracting Telescopes

Refracting telescopes are optical telescopes that use only lenses. At one end of a closed tube is an **objective lens**. This is the lens closest to the object being viewed, and it is always convex. This lens gathers light from distant objects and bends the light to a focal plane—a place where light from a lens comes together—at the other end of the tube. There the eyepiece lens acts like a magnifying glass, making the image look larger. The eyepiece lens can be convex or concave. If it's convex, everything looks upside down.

Professional astronomers rarely look through their telescopes, so they don't use eyepieces. Instead, they record the images, either on film or with **charge-coupled devices** (CCDs). A CCD is a close relative of the device that takes pictures in a digital camera.

One of the major problems with refractors is **aberration**. An aberration is a misshapen image or one with colored edges.

Galileo's refractors made images with rainbow coloring around the edges. This happened because a convex lens slows down different colors of light passing through it by different amounts. For instance, it slows violet light more than it slows red light.

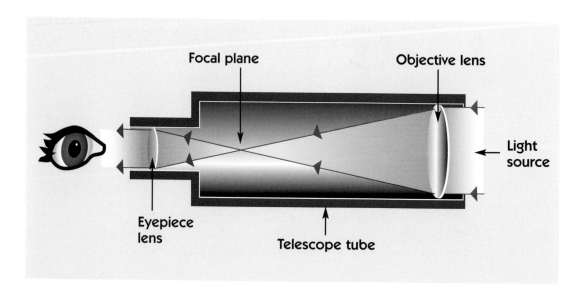

Focal plane   Objective lens

Light source

Eyepiece lens

Telescope tube

Reflecting Telescopes

Sir Isaac Newton invented the first reflecting telescope in 1680. This optical telescope uses curved mirrors instead of lenses. Light is collected by one concave primary mirror and reflected forward to a secondary mirror. The second mirror reflects the light rays out through the side of the tube to an eyepiece, camera, or CCD. Since all wavelengths of light are reflected equally by a mirror, there is no color distortion.

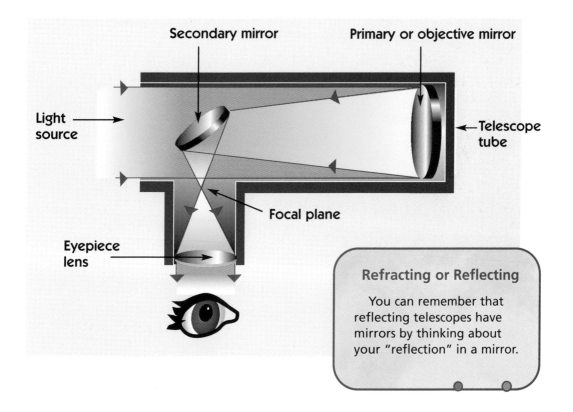

Refracting or Reflecting

You can remember that reflecting telescopes have mirrors by thinking about your "reflection" in a mirror.

Gathering Light

How much light a telescope gathers depends on the **aperture**, or diameter, of the objective lens or primary mirror. Larger apertures gather more light to each image point, making a brighter final image.

chapter 3

Surface to Space

Have you ever looked at the sky through a telescope? If so, you probably fixed on the Moon so you could take a closer look at its "face." You probably saw craters and mountains.

Professional astronomers use telescopes to do the same thing—to look at distant objects in finer detail. They also use them to gather light for **spectrographs**.

A spectrograph breaks up light and spreads it into its different colors. Bands of spread-out light are called *spectra* (think rainbows). Astronomers study spectra to discover the chemical makeup, motion, and temperature of stars, planets, and gas clouds.

Finding distant objects and showing them in detail depends on the diameter of the main mirror or lens. Gigantic optical telescopes can gather about 1 million times more light than the eye alone. In other words, these telescopes can find objects 1 million times fainter than the unaided eye can see.

This spectrum of our Sun was created with the Fourier Transform Spectrometer at Kitt Peak National Observatory near Tucson, Arizona.

Refractors or Reflectors

The Lick Observatory at the University of California in Santa Cruz, California, houses a 36-inch refracting telescope, which has been in operation since 1888. The Yerkes Observatory at the University of Chicago in Williams Bay, Wisconsin, has a 40-inch refractor. These are the largest refracting telescopes in operation today.

Since the lenses can only be supported around their edges, a very large lens will bend under its own weight. So the largest modern telescopes are reflectors, using mirrors that are completely supported from behind.

Most telescopes used by amateur astronomers have objective lenses with diameters of 4 to 8 inches. Professional astronomers use reflectors with mirrors that measure more than 60 inches in diameter. The first telescope to use a mirror that big was built in 1908 on Mount Wilson near Pasadena, California.

From 1948 to 1976, the world's largest reflector was the Hale Telescope, with a 200-inch mirror. This telescope is housed at the Palomar Observatory near San Diego, California. In 1976, the Soviet Union's 236-inch reflector began operating in the Caucasus Mountains in Russia.

Then in 1978, a new generation of telescopes began to appear. Like large lenses, extremely large mirrors can bend or warp under their own weight. The new designs overcame the size limitations.

Palomar Observatory

New Designs for Reflectors

Spin-Cast Mirrors

An advanced technique called *spin casting* helped create the new thin-disk mirrors. A giant rotating oven spins melted glass at controlled speeds. The liquid glass flows into perfect shapes for telescope mirrors.

Thin-disk mirrors are light for their size. Telescopes that use these mirrors have computer systems that constantly adjust the mirrors to keep them correctly shaped.

This design is used in the four individual telescopes that together make up the Very Large Telescope (VLT) located on Cerro Paranal, Chile. Each has a mirror 27 feet in diameter and only 7 inches thick. When all four telescopes focus on the same object, they have the light-gathering power of a single telescope with a mirror 52 feet in diameter.

Honeycomb Mirrors

Honeycomb mirrors are made by pouring melted glass into a mold filled with hundreds of **hexagonal** blocks. The liquid glass covers the blocks and fills the spaces between them. After the glass cools and hardens, the blocks are removed. What's left is a hard glass structure so light that it can float on water.

This design was used by astronomers at the University of Arizona's Steward Observatory to build a mirror 27½ feet in diameter. It is the first of twin mirrors being built on Mount Graham in Arizona. When construction is completed, the mirrors will be mounted side by side, like a giant pair of binoculars. In fact, this telescope is called the Large Binocular Telescope (LBT).

Steward Observatory

Segmented Mirrors

Segmented mirrors are actually several smaller mirrors that work together to do the job of one larger mirror. Keck I and Keck II Telescopes, located on Mauna Kea in Hawaii, have segmented mirrors. Each is a **mosaic** of 36 hexagonal mirrors mounted close together. Together, they form a reflecting surface about 33 feet in diameter. Twice per second, a computer-controlled sensor system adjusts each mirror to keep it in exactly the right position.

A dozen observatories dot the 13,800-foot summit of Mauna Kea, a mountain on the island of Hawaii. Because of its location, surrounded by miles of temperate ocean with no other nearby mountains to throw dust into the air, the atmosphere above the Mauna Kea observatory is clear, calm, and dry most of the time.

The Kecks' mirrors have 4 times the light-gathering ability of the Hale telescope on Mt. Palomar and 17 times that of the Hubble Space Telescope. The Hubble can see a bit more clearly, but the Kecks can see farther and gather

Keck Telescopes

scientific data on objects so dim that they are beyond the reach of any other telescope.

The two are working together, however. When the space-based Hubble finds distant objects of interest, teams of scientists extend the exploration farther using the land-based Kecks. This new idea of using both space and land-based telescopes is unlocking many secrets of the universe.

Keck astronomers are discovering new galaxies and searching our own Milky Way for new planetary systems. They are studying stars—living, dying, and exploding. As they continue to probe space deeper, they may even discover life beyond our own planet.

chapter 4

Dishes and Antennae

It was 1931. Physicist Karl Jansky was busy in his lab. He worked for Bell Telephone, and the company was looking for ways to make transatlantic telephone service possible. They considered using shortwave radio signals and asked Jansky to look for sources of static that could interfere.

Shortwaves carry FM radio broadcasts, television signals, and transoceanic telephone conversations. Shortwave radios are used by pilots, amateur radio operators, police officers, taxi drivers, and others to send and receive messages.

Physicist Karl Jansky is pointing to a position on a chart where he first recorded radio noise from space.

Jansky built a radio telescope and mounted it on a turntable. By rotating the telescope, he could point it in any direction. After a few months, he found three sources of static—close thunderstorms; distant thunderstorms; and a strange, faint hiss.

After a year of study, Jansky found the hiss was radiation coming from somewhere in the Milky Way. He wanted to continue to study these radio waves, but Bell Telephone had its answer and assigned Jansky to other projects. Grote Reber took over where Jansky left off.

First radio telescope built by Karl Jansky

In 1937, Reber built the first bowl-shaped radio telescope in his backyard. His telescope was a mirror made of sheet metal 31 feet in diameter.

Using radio telescopes, astronomers have also discovered objects missed by optical telescopes. These include pulsars, which are collapsed stars that emit radio waves in regular pulses, and quasars, which are very distant, starlike objects that give off huge amounts of radiation.

Reber's studies with his radio telescope led to the discovery that the Sun and the center of our Milky Way galaxy were strong sources of radio waves. Strong radio waves were also detected from dark areas of space. Scientists later learned these sources are the leftovers of exploded stars and distant galaxies.

Modern radio telescopes work much like Reber's. They collect radio waves with a large reflector, or dish antenna. The dish has the same shape as the mirror of a reflecting telescope, only much larger.

The reflector focuses the waves onto a small, central antenna that turns them into electric signals. The antenna sends the signals to a receiver, which **amplifies** them and sends them to a computer. The computer analyzes the radio waves and creates an image of their source.

Reber's backyard telescope

Most radio telescopes have motors that turn them toward objects in the sky that emit radio signals. The largest moving-dish telescopes—one in Germany and one in West Virginia—measure 330 feet in diameter. But the world's largest radio telescope doesn't turn or have a motor. This fixed-dish telescope is located in Arecibo, Puerto Rico. It is 1000 feet across and takes up an entire valley! Scientists use this and other large fixed-dish radio telescopes to study pulsars and other galaxies.

Radio telescopes have allowed us to explore new areas of the universe because radio waves penetrate dust and gas through which light can't travel. The low-energy radio wavelengths are much longer than the wavelengths of visible light. Because of that, even the largest radio telescopes produce rather blurry images.

Astronomers have developed a new system called radio **interferometry**. It works by taking radio signals from several different telescopes and concentrating them to produce an extremely sharp image. This works best with many dishes spread out over long distances.

A collection of dishes is known as an array. One array, known as the Very Large Array (VLA), was built on a high plain near Socorro, New Mexico, in the 1970s. The VLA has 27 radio telescopes, spread out over

24 miles. Each 82-foot dish is attached to rails and movable. The entire Y-shaped array can point to any part of the sky

Interferometry

Interferometry is also used with optical telescopes. The twin Keck telescopes use this process to view the dimmer of the two stars of a binary. An animated explanation is given on Planet Quest at **http://planetquest.jpl.nasa.gov/Keck/keck_index.html.**

and focus on a large object or, using higher **resolution**, on a smaller one.

The sharpest radio images come from the Very Long Baseline Array (VLBA). The VLBA is the world's largest astronomical instrument. The system of ten 82-foot dishes stretches over 5000 U.S. miles—from the Virgin Islands north to New Hampshire and west to Hawaii. This powerful system helps scientists study the cores of faraway quasars and take the measurements of the speed of debris from exploding stars.

Working together, the VLBA telescopes equal a single dish, with a diameter about the same as Earth's diameter. Now that's some kind of dish!

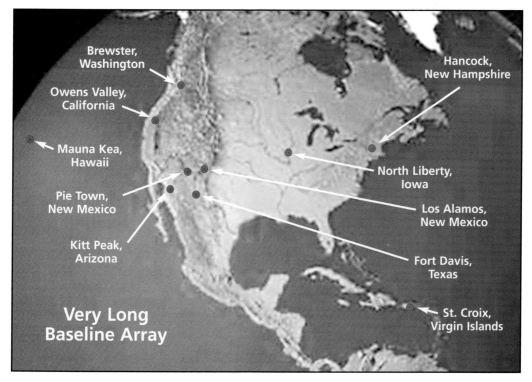

Brewster, Washington

Owens Valley, California

Mauna Kea, Hawaii

Pie Town, New Mexico

Kitt Peak, Arizona

Hancock, New Hampshire

North Liberty, Iowa

Los Alamos, New Mexico

Fort Davis, Texas

St. Croix, Virgin Islands

Very Long Baseline Array

chapter 5

Beyond Visible Light

Infrared Telescopes

Have you ever used night-vision equipment or seen how it works in movies or on TV? Night-vision equipment finds objects in the dark by focusing on the heat in the form of the infrared rays they emit. Almost any room-temperature object gives off **thermal** radiation.

People and other warm-blooded creatures glow brightly with infrared rays. Police and firefighters use special cameras to find people in dark, foggy, or smoke-filled places. Soldiers use the same kind of cameras to "see" the exhaust from tanks or aircraft at night. And astronomers use infrared equipment to find stars just beginning to form in clouds of dust and gas.

To work, infrared telescopes need two things.

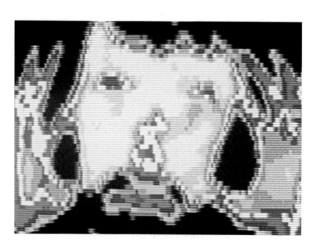

Close-up view of a face on a monitor that was taken with an infrared video camera

First, they must be kept cold, since any room-temperature object—including the telescope itself—gives off infrared rays, which could interfere with infrared radiation coming from space.

The second thing they need is to be located at high altitudes. Water in the air absorbs many infrared rays. To avoid this, astronomers build infrared telescopes on mountains where the air is thin and dry. Infrared scopes are also sent into space aboard satellites.

Other Telescopes

The Earth's atmosphere almost completely blocks ultraviolet (UV), X-ray, and gamma ray radiation coming from space. Telescopes used to detect these parts of the EM spectrum are placed on spacecraft that orbit above the atmosphere.

Because these types of rays carry so much energy, the telescopes that detect them look very different from optical telescopes. The mirrors they have are very strange—if they have mirrors at all.

The Hopkins Ultraviolet Telescope (HUT) is part of the Astro Observatory, which orbited Earth as **payload** in two **space shuttles** (1990 and 1995). The HUT can detect light waves too short to be seen by the Hubble Space Telescope.

UV Telescopes

A bowl-shaped mirror reflects most UV rays—all except those with the shortest wavelengths. Short-wavelength UV rays will only reflect off a mirror positioned at a certain angle. This is called a *grazing incidence*.

So why would anyone want to study "sunburn" rays? Because some of the hottest, young stars in the universe are only visible in the ultraviolet band of the spectrum. Astronomers also use UV telescopes to study quasars and white dwarfs, the very hot remnants of lighter stars that have died.

Grazing Incidence

Have you ever skipped stones? You know how you have to get the angle just right for the rock to bounce off the water's surface instead of sinking? That is how rays reflect at a grazing incidence.

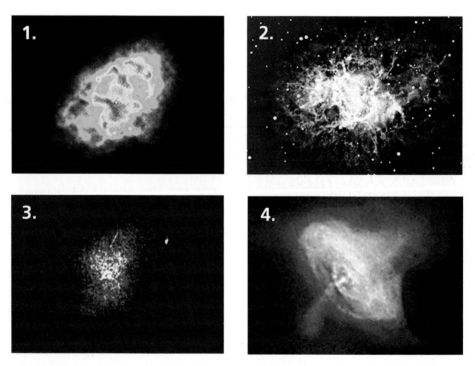

The Crab Nebula seen through four different telescopes: 1. Radio, National Radio Astronomy Observatory; 2. Visible, Hale Telescope; 3. Far Ultraviolet, Ultraviolet Imaging Telescope; 4. X-ray, Chandra X-ray Observatory

X-ray Telescopes

You know X rays can pass through your skin and flesh so doctors can look inside your body. Just like the rays pass through flesh, most X rays can pass straight through lenses and mirrors. As a result, X-ray telescopes don't have mirrors.

Most X-ray telescopes have iron or lead slats. Often they find X rays given off by collapsed stars, or neutron stars. Sometimes they find telltale signs of black holes, areas in space no eye can see because the gravity is so strong that not even light can escape.

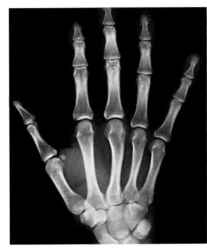

X ray of a human hand

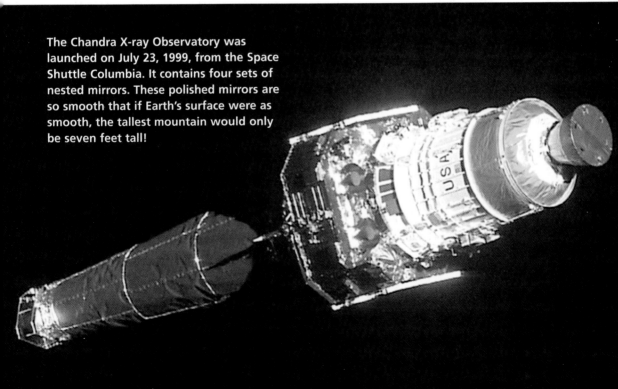

The Chandra X-ray Observatory was launched on July 23, 1999, from the Space Shuttle Columbia. It contains four sets of nested mirrors. These polished mirrors are so smooth that if Earth's surface were as smooth, the tallest mountain would only be seven feet tall!

chapter 6

In Orbit

Scorpius X-1

In 1949, early rockets were launched above Earth's atmosphere. Radiation detectors aboard discovered X rays coming from the Sun. Thirteen years later in 1962, a team of scientists at American Science and Engineering (AS&E) in Cambridge, Massachusetts, used a small X-ray detector aboard an Aerobee rocket to discover Scorpius X-1. This was the first source of X rays outside our solar system. Scientists wanted to know more!

Scorpius X-1

Scorpius X-1 is more than 9000 light-years from Earth, one-third of the way to the center of the Milky Way. The binary system is composed of a dense neutron star and a smaller star much like our Sun.

AS&E engineers made the first imaging X-ray telescope in 1963. It rode on a small rocket and created images of hot spots in the Sun's upper atmosphere. This telescope was about the same size as the optical telescope Galileo used in 1610.

With the launch of the first human-made satellites, our understanding of space increased dramatically. These satellites are orbiting machines that have many different jobs to do, including carrying telescopes for scientific research.

All satellites, whatever their jobs, have two main parts—the payload and the **bus**. The payload is all the equipment the satellite needs to do its job— telescopes, antennas, cameras, radar equipment, and more. The bus is the part of the satellite that carries all the equipment and provides electrical power.

In the 1970s, the Uhuru X-ray Satellite made some spectacular discoveries. This satellite was the first Earth-orbiting mission to focus on just X rays. Sponsored by the National Aeronautics and Space Administration (NASA), this early X-ray telescope carried simple equipment. Its X-ray sensor was little more than a **Geiger counter** attached to a viewing tube to locate the X-ray sources. Uhuru found black holes, neutron stars, and vast regions of superheated interstellar gases.

For the next 30 years, a series of orbiting observatories made increasingly interesting discoveries. They included Skylab, which was launched in the early 1970s. Aboard Skylab, three different crews of three people each conducted UV experiments and detailed X-ray studies of the Sun.

Skylab in orbit around Earth

Skylab

On July 11, 1979, the empty Skylab fell to Earth. Debris was scattered over the Indian Ocean and a sparsely populated region of Western Australia.

Skylab soon led to the Einstein Observatory, which was launched in 1978 carrying the largest X-ray telescope ever built. NASA's Einstein found over 7000 sources of X rays and made the first X-ray images of shock waves from exploding stars.

In 1990, the Roentgensatellite (ROSAT) carried an even larger X-ray telescope into space. ROSAT was built and operated jointly by Germany, England, and the United States. It has since located over 60,000 sources of cosmic X rays.

Then in 1999, NASA used the Space Shuttle Columbia to launch Chandra X-ray Observatory. Chandra is the third of NASA's Great Observatories. It joined the Hubble Space Telescope (HST), launched in 1990, and the Compton Gamma Ray Observatory, launched in 1991.

Chandra's bus has solar panels to power its electronics, a temperature-control system to keep the telescope cool, and a communications system to send information to scientists on Earth. Its payload consists of the telescope and instruments to make images of the X rays. The scope itself has four pairs of nesting mirrors. They are the largest, most perfectly shaped, and smoothest mirrors ever made.

In 1981, NASA launched the first space shuttle. The Columbia flew 28 missions. Sadly, the Columbia and its crew were lost during re-entry on February 1, 2003.

Chandra Trivia

- Chandra can see X rays emitted by particles just before they fall into a black hole.

- Chandra can observe X rays given off by gas clouds so wide that it would take light five million years to travel from one side to the other.

- If your eyes could see as clearly as Chandra does, you could read a sign 12 miles away.

- Some of the light that Chandra sees has been traveling through space for 10 billion years.

- Chandra operates on about the same amount of power as a hair dryer does.

Eastman Kodak technicians placing Chandra into a vertical position

Chandra finds and forms images of X-ray sources billions of light-years away from Earth. Its images are 25 times sharper than those from the best X-ray telescope to go into space before it. Chandra's resolving power is about the same as a telescope that would let you read newsprint ½ mile away.

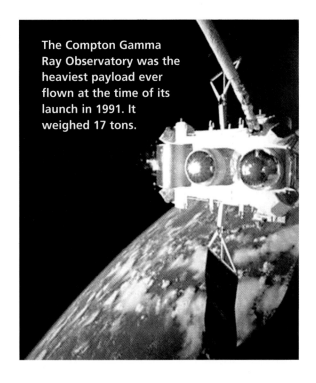

The Compton Gamma Ray Observatory was the heaviest payload ever flown at the time of its launch in 1991. It weighed 17 tons.

This resolving power allows more detailed studies of black holes, supernovas, and dark matter in deep space. Chandra's imagery of the Crab Nebula, for instance, shows details optical imagery can't match.

In the four centuries between Galileo's telescope and the Hubble Space Telescope, optical scopes improved in sensitivity by 100 million times. The Chandra X-ray Observatory achieved the same sensitivity improvement over the first X-ray telescope, but in only 28 years.

Chandra's sibling, the Compton Gamma Ray Observatory (CGRO), was launched in April 1991. This artificial satellite studied gamma rays from space with its four telescopes.

By March 2000, the CGRO had delivered information four years beyond what was expected. At that time, NASA scientists discovered one of the CGRO's three controlling systems wasn't working. Since there was a possibility that debris from the falling satellite might pose a risk to people on Earth, NASA decided to bring the satellite down.

Three months later, engineers on the ground turned the Compton Gamma Ray Observatory toward its home planet. Most of it burned up as it reentered Earth's atmosphere. The rest splashed down somewhere in the Pacific Ocean. The CGRO's mission was officially over.

chapter 7

Orbiting Opticals

So what if you could take a huge optical telescope, add infrared and ultraviolet capabilities, and put it in orbit beyond Earth's atmosphere? Well, NASA did just that.

The first of NASA's Great Observatories was launched in 1990 by the Space Shuttle Discovery. Discovery lifted the Hubble Space Telescope (HST) into space and placed it into orbit some 380 miles above Earth. There, light is not distorted or absorbed by our planet's atmosphere. As a result, the HST has returned some incredible space images.

The Hubble is a reflector. It gathers rays and sends information back to the Goddard Space Flight Center in Greenbelt, Maryland. From there the information travels to the Space Telescope Science Institute in Baltimore, Maryland, where it is turned back into pictures and astronomical data.

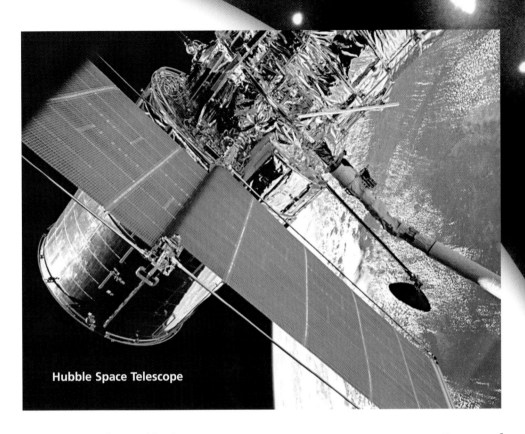

Hubble Space Telescope

- The Wide Field Planetary Camera is HST's main camera. It is used to observe everything from planets to objects outside our galaxy. If you've seen photos from the Hubble, they were probably taken with this camera.

- The Advanced Camera for Surveys was installed in March 2002. This camera is used to observe weather on other planets, conduct surveys of the universe, and study the makeup of galaxies.

- The Near Infrared Camera and Multi-Object Spectrometer is sensitive to infrared light. It is used to observe objects, such as new star beds hidden by gas and dust, and to look into deepest space.

- The Space Telescope Imaging Spectrograph separates cosmic light into different colors of the spectrum.

- The Fine Guidance Sensors keep HST pointed in the right direction by targeting certain stars and locking onto them.

The first true-color image of Jupiter was captured by the Hubble Space Telescope's Wide Field Planetary Camera.

Hubble's mirrors are made of special warp-resistant glass and are kept at a nearly constant 70°F. They are coated with an ultrathin layer of pure aluminum and another extremely thin layer of magnesium fluoride. The magnesium helps reflect ultraviolet light.

The mirrors are very smooth and almost perfect curves. In fact, if HST's primary mirror were blown up to the size of Earth, its biggest bump would only be six inches high.

Not long after Hubble's launch, scientists found a flaw in its primary mirror. The aberration made images fuzzy because some of the collected light was scattered. The problem happened because the outer edge of the mirror was ground too flat. It seems hard to believe, but the error was only four **microns** deep—around 1/50 the thickness of a human hair!

Engineers got busy and made "eyeglasses" for Hubble. In 1993, Space Shuttle Endeavor astronauts carried the corrective optics mirrors to the orbiting HST and connected them to the Wide Field Planetary Camera. This corrected the aberration and sharpened the images.

What has Hubble found so far? Gigantic young star clusters, formed in the collisions of galaxies. Massive black holes. Scars and plumes from the impact of comets on Jupiter. Galaxies on the outer edges of the observable universe. Accurate distances to stars in a far galaxy. And much, much more. After a final servicing by shuttle astronauts in 2005, the HST will be outfitted with the most scientific instruments ever flown in space.

Hubble Trivia

- Hubble travels about 5 miles per second, or 18,000 mph. It would take the HST only 10 minutes to go from Los Angeles to New York City.
- Hubble completes one orbit every 97 minutes.
- Hubble can change the direction it's pointing by 90 degrees in 15 minutes. That's the same as the movement of a minute hand on a clock.
- During one orbit, Hubble uses about the same amount of energy as 24 100-watt lightbulbs.
- Hubble averages three observations an hour. Each observation requires more than 100 computer functions.
- Hubble produces more than 10 billion bits of scientific data per week.
- Hubble can steadily and accurately focus on a target for 24 hours. That's the same as holding a laser beam on a dime that is almost 200 miles away.

In 2010, the James Webb Space Telescope (formerly known as the Next Generation Space Telescope) is expected to be launched. It will take almost three months to reach its destination about 940,000 miles above Earth. Unlike Hubble, space shuttle astronauts will not service the James Webb Space Telescope because it will be too far away.

Webb is designed to make observations in the far-visible to the mid-infrared part of the spectrum. This wavelength coverage is different from that of the HST, which covers the range from the ultraviolet to the near-infrared. The Webb will have a primary mirror diameter more than twice as large as HST, giving it much more light-gathering capability and much greater resolution.

chapter 8

Into the Beyond

The only way to learn more about the beyond than what orbiting observatories can tell us is to travel there. Seventy-five years ago, we might have said "Impossible!" But today, we are on our way.

Rangers

Between 1961 and 1965, NASA launched nine unmanned space vehicles, called *probes*, in the Ranger project. This project gave us our first up close look at the Moon. Rangers 7, 8, and 9 sent more than 17,000 photos of the Moon's surface before crash-landing on the Moon.

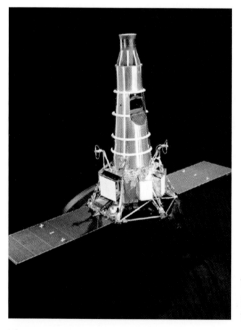

The fleet of Ranger spacecraft provided the first live television transmissions from the Moon.

Vikings

A decade later, NASA launched
Vikings 1 and 2 within a couple of weeks
of each other. These unmanned probes
traveled to Mars. It took them only ten months to
get there, and once they did, they went into orbit
around the red planet. When the orbiting probes found
suitable places to set down, the landers were released.
Instruments aboard measured the atmosphere, took soil
samples, and looked for signs of life. If extraterrestrial life existed,
the Vikings found no sign of it.

Viking 1 took this picture of the Martian
surface and sky on July 24, 1976. Part of
the spacecraft is visible in the foreground.

Saturn and its moon Titan as photographed by Pioneer 11

Pioneers

In 1972, Pioneer 10 was launched, and it safely maneuvered through an asteroid belt on its way to Jupiter. There, it took the first up close photos of Jupiter and found the planet to be mostly liquid and gas.

Pioneer 10 continued its journey to the outer portion of our solar system, studying solar wind and cosmic rays entering our galaxy from other parts of the universe. In 1995, it became the first human-made object to leave the solar system. Its mission officially ended in 1997.

Pioneer 11, launched in 1973, zipped by Jupiter and sped toward Saturn. It reached the ringed planet in 1979. Pioneer 11 took close-ups of the planet and its rings and found its moon, Titan, was too cold for life as we know it.

Pioneer 11 continued to the outer parts of our solar system well beyond Pluto. Communication with the probe stopped in 1995 when the probe's power was too low to operate its instruments and transmit data.

Scientists don't know if Pioneer 11 is continuing its scheduled journey to the constellation Aquila. If it is, it will take some 4 million years to reach there. Pioneer 10 travels toward Aldebaran, in the Taurus constellation. The red star is 68 light-years away. If Pioneer 10 is successful, it will reach Aldebaran in 2 million years. On January 23, 2003, Pioneer 10 sent its last signal to Earth.

> ### Pioneer Trivia
>
> A plaque with a drawing of a man, a woman, and the location of the Sun and Earth in the Milky Way is onboard each craft. They are meant as greetings for any extraterrestrials that might find the probes.

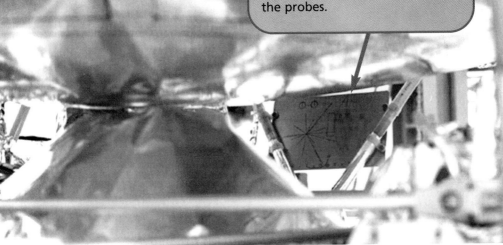

Plaque attached to one of the Pioneer probes

Voyagers

The Pioneers were followed by the Voyagers. Voyager 1 launched on September 5, 1977. It flew past Jupiter in March 1979, reaching Saturn in November 1980.

Voyager 2 left Earth on August 20, 1977. Though it launched a month earlier than Voyager 1, it traveled slower, passing Jupiter in July 1979. Voyager 2 passed Saturn and Neptune on its way to Uranus, which it reached in 1986.

The Voyager duo, recently renamed Voyager Interstellar Mission, told scientists many previously unknown things about the outer planets. They found

- cloud formations around Jupiter.
- volcanic activity on Io, one of Jupiter's moons.
- that besides its rings, Saturn has several thousand smaller "ringlets."
- that Uranus has ten more moons than we thought and an extreme magnetic field.
- that Neptune has three rings and six previously unseen moons.

The Voyager probes are still traveling toward deep space, sending back information on the far reaches of our solar system.

Galileo Probe

Galileo

Launched in 1989, Galileo flew past our Moon and the asteroids called Gaspra and Ida. The probe even found a natural satellite orbiting Ida. Galileo successfully went into orbit around Jupiter in 1995. The satellite has sent back the closest images of the planet ever taken. By the end of 2002, Galileo was almost out of fuel, so scientists set it on a course to crash into Jupiter.

Probes like these will some day tell scientists likely places to set up housekeeping in space. Early space stations like Skylab and the Russian Mir have already housed astronauts, engineers, and other scientists as they conducted experiments while in orbit around Earth. Both outlived their missions, but new space stations will replace them. From those jumping-off spots, a whole new universe of possibilities will open.

A Final Word

When the Space Infrared Telescope Facility (SIRTF) launches in 2003, it will join other great observatories. Each views the universe in a different kind of light—visible, infrared, gamma rays, and X rays. The James Webb Space Telescope will join them and eventually replace the aging Hubble.

Together, these orbiting observatories will help scientists discover

- how galaxies formed in the early universe.
- how stars and planetary systems form and evolve.
- whether habitable or life-bearing planets exist around nearby stars.
- how life forms and evolves.

On February 11, 2003, NASA released the best picture ever taken of the universe as a baby. The Wilkinson Microwave Anisotropy Probe (WMAP) captured the oldest light in the universe, enabling scientists to place the age of the universe at 13.7 billion years.

What new data will scientists find? How will it help us on our journey into the future?

Internet Sites

http://www.nasa.gov/

Learning has never been so much fun. Click on the link for kids or students to find out the latest news from NASA, plan a trip to Mars, or search for a topic of interest on the National Aeronautics and Space Administration site.

http://hubble.gsfc.nasa.gov/overview

Visit this site for current information about the Hubble Satellite. You can also track the Hubble's path in orbit.

http://mo-www.harvard.edu/MicroObservatory

An excellent source for viewing current telescopic pictures of space.

http://starchild.gsfc.nasa.gov/docs/StarChild/StarChild.html

This Learning Center for Young Astronomers has two levels for kids. Search the site for more information on the topics you read about in this book.

http://www.nationalgeographic.com/features/97/stars/index.html

Star Journey provides some incredible photos, taken by the Hubble Telescope, of the Milky Way and other galaxies.

http://science.howstuffworks.com/telescope.htm

Find out how telescopes work and find directions for building a simple telescope of your own.

http://seds.lpl.arizona.edu/nineplanets/nineplanets/spacecraft.html

This Web page provides a listing of spacecraft that have conducted past research and continue to conduct ongoing research in space.

http://science.nasa.gov/headlines/y2003/11feb_map.htm

Visit this NASA site and see images of the oldest light in the universe.

Books

The letters *RL* in the brackets indicate the reading level of the book listed. *IL* indicates the approximate interest level. Perfection Learning's catalog numbers are included for your ordering convenience. *PB* indicates paperback. *CC* indicates Cover Craft. *HB* indicates hardcover.

Astronomy by Kristen Lippincott. Enhanced by well-captioned color photographs and drawings, the text conveys the excitement of discovery—the planets, space exploration, supernovas, and black holes. Dorling Kindersley, 1994. [RL 8 IL 3–8] (5868006 HB)

Everyday Astronomy by Jon Kirkwood. This book explores the world of astronomy, discussing planets, stars, meteors, comets, galaxies, and more. Millbrook Press, 1998. [RL 5 IL 4–8] (3111406 HB)

Exploring Space by Jon Kirkwood. Fantastic images and revealing text allow readers to explore the wonders of the cosmos, while experiments let them study the size and scale of the universe in which we live. Millbrook Press, 1999. [RL 5 IL 4–8] (3111506 HB)

Space: A Nonfiction Companion to *Midnight on the Moon* by Will Osborne & Mary Pope Osborne. This is a research guide to the secrets of the universe. It includes information on stars, planets, space travel, life on other planets, and much more. Random House, 2002. [RL 2.8 IL 1–6] (3370901 PB)

Space Exploration by Carole Stott. This book is devoted to examining the rockets, landers, and shuttles that have made space exploration possible. Dorling Kindersley, 1997. [RL 6.5 IL 5–9] (5867406 HB)

The Universe by Seymour Simon. Breathtaking photos show everything from the birth of a star to a galaxy far beyond ours. HarperCollins, 1998. [RL 5.5 IL 1–6] (3276901 PB 3276902 CC)

Glossary

aberration   (ab uh RAY shun) defect in a lens or mirror that causes a distorted image or one with colored edges

amplify   (AM pluh feye) to increase the magnitude of a signal

aperture   (AP uh cher) the diameter of lens or mirror that gathers light

apparent   (uh PAIR uhnt) appearing to show particular qualities or attributes that may not be true

bus   (buhs) part of a space exploration vehicle

charge-coupled device   (charj KUH puhld div ICE) type of digital camera containing an array of extremely light-sensitive electrical parts

concave   (kahn KAYV) having a surface that curves inward

convex   (kahn VEKS) having a surface that curves outward

electromagnetic radiation   (il ek troh mag NET ik ray dee AY shuhn) light energy

emit   (ee MIT) to give off

Geiger counter   (GEYE ger KOWN ter) instrument used to detect and measure the levels of radiation from a radioactive substance

hexagonal   (heks AH gon uhl) having six straight sides and six angles

interferometry (in ter fuh RAW muh tree) use of device called an *interferometer* to analyze waves

micron (MEYE krahn) unit of measurement equal to one millionth of a meter

mosaic (moh ZAY ik) light-sensitive surface made of small pieces that converts incoming light into an electric charge

nuclei (NOO klee eye) plural of nucleus; central or most important part that has others grouped or built around it

objective lens (ahb JEK tiv lenz) telescope lens that is closest to the object being viewed

optical (AHP tik uhl) relating to light that can be seen

payload (PAY lohd) instruments or passengers carried by a spacecraft

reflect (ri FLEKT) to redirect something that strikes a surface, especially light, sound, or heat

refract (ri FRAKT) bend and alter the course of a wave of energy as it passes through something

resolution (rez uh LOO shun) quality and sharpness of an image

segmented (SEG men tuhd) divided into sections

space shuttle (spays SHUH tuhl) reusable spacecraft designed to transport people and cargo between Earth and space

spectrograph (SPEK truh graf) instrument used to obtain a visual record of a spectrum (see separate glossary entry)

spectrum (SPEK truhm) band or range of radiation

speed of light   (speed uhv leyet)   speed at which light energy moves through a vacuum, about 186,000 miles per second

thermal   (THER muhl)   having to do with heat

wavelength   (WAYV length)   distance between two consecutive peaks or troughs, or low points, on a wave

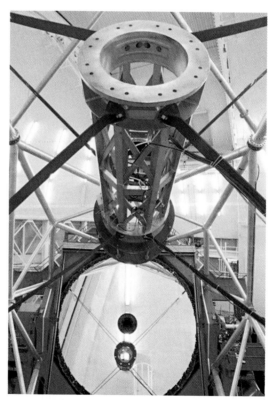

Looking down at the primary mirror in the interior of the Gemini North Telescope in Mauna Kea, Hawaii

Index